CHESS
BASICS

CHESS
BASICS

The quickest way
to learn to play
(and win)

NIGEL SHORT

PUZZLE
WRIGHT
PRESS

New York

Special thanks to Daniel King, International Grandmaster and friend, without whom this book would not have been possible.

PUZZLE WRIGHT PRESS
New York

An Imprint of Sterling Publishing Co., Inc.

PUZZLEWRIGHT PRESS and the distinctive Puzzlewright Press logo are registered trademarks of Sterling Publishing Co., Inc.

First published in Great Britain in 1993 by Stanley Paul and Company Limited
First published in the United States in 1994 by Sterling Publishing Co., Inc.

ISBN 978-1-4549-4442-3

Distributed in Canada by Sterling Publishing Co., Inc.
c/o Canadian Manda Group, 664 Annette Street
Toronto, Ontario M6S 2C8, Canada

For information about custom editions, special sales, and premium and corporate purchases, please contact Sterling Special Sales at 800-805-5489 or specialsales@sterlingpublishing.com.

Manufactured in the United States of America

2   4   6   8   10   9   7   5   3   1

sterlingpublishing.com
puzzlewright.com

Cover photograph by Andrii Sedykh/iStock/Getty Images Plus
Cover design by Igor Satanovsky
Designed by Martin Lovelock
Photographs by Colin Walton
Diagrams by Graham Douglas

Contents

Foreword

Chess is many things to me; my passion for it has been so consuming that at many times I've forgotten to eat and sleep. It has given me a bond with people from diverse backgrounds: the young lady from Ulan Bator; the Ukrainian officer on the Iraq/Kuwait border; the prisoner in Wormwood Scrubs. Chess has also been my official profession for eleven years and, unofficially, for a good many years before that. But most of all, chess is my friend.

I began to play chess at the age of five. This is not at all an unusual age for a young player to begin, although I was extremely fortunate that my later career was not wrecked before it started. I remember watching my father one day demonstrate the chess moves to my older brother. When he had tired of defeat, I asked whether I, too, could be permitted a game. My father replied that I was too young, and had it not been for my mother's intervention, it is possible that my contact with chess would have ended then and there. Fortunately, that didn't happen and my love affair with the game began.

It wasn't until two years later, however, that I began to get more seriously involved in the noble sport. It was 1972 and the time of the great Fischer-Spassky World Championship match in Reykjavik. This superpower tussle at the height of the Cold War captured the public's imagination. Yet it was not the politics that interested me, but the battle of the sixty-four squares. I joined my first club at that time, played in my first tournament and loved every moment. I hope that, with the aid of this book, you will enjoy the game as much as I do.

Welcome to the world of chess.

Nigel Short

About the Game

At World Championship level, chess in its purest form is the
ultimate struggle between two minds. But the main attraction of
this ancient game is that it is enjoyed by players of all ages and
nationalities – professionals, enthusiasts and occasional players.
What is even more appealing about chess is that even beginners
can quickly master it with enough confidence to challenge more
experienced players to a game. So long as you have some time to
spare, a chess set (or, these days, perhaps even a computer), there
is nothing to prevent you from learning how to play, trying to
improve on your last efforts or exploring new ways to defeat your
opponent on the chessboard. If your concentration is at its best
during a game, you can achieve an almost trance-like state in
which all sense of time is lost and the minutes simply fly by.

Perhaps chess is the most satisfying of games because, if you
win, it is you alone who takes the credit. For the same reason, it
is also the hardest game if you lose. In backgammon, you can
always blame the dice; if you lose at football, you can blame your
team-mates; but in chess only you and the person you are playing
are responsible for the outcome of a game.

THE ORIGINS OF THE GAME
The earliest evidence of chess dates back to the 5th century AD,
when it 'emerged' in India (exactly when and how it was invented
is unclear). From there, the game quickly spread to Persia (now
Iran), and then on to the Arab world. Chess finally reached
Europe in the 10th century, as a result of Arab expansion, where
it soon became popular among the upper classes. At that time,
they were the only ones who could afford the luxury of spending
hours over a chessboard. In the later Middle Ages, as the
merchant classes established themselves, the game was gradually
taken up by them. This was, if you like, the beginning of the
democratization of chess, which has culminated in the game we
know today, when anyone who wants to play the game *can* do so
(provided, of course, that they know all the moves and so on).

At every stage of its development, chess has mirrored the society in which it has been played; at first there were small adaptations to the rules and later the different philosophies behind the game were adapted to suit the times. Not surprisingly, the widespread introduction of new technology has had a profound effect on the game. These days, an essential part of every professional chess' player's baggage is a lap-top computer with the facility to contain thousands of games and which can recall in an instant all the previous games of an opponent who is to be challenged. Computers which also play chess are rapidly being improved and there will no doubt come a time when they are readily accepted by professional chess players.

BEFORE YOU LEARN TO PLAY

Whether you are a novice – or want to improve your existing game – remember that chess only seems difficult to those who are unfamiliar with the moves and rules. It's true that the various permutations are endless, but once you have learned how to play, trying to beat a particular player can become an absorbing and fascinating challenge for the mind. Try to read through this book from the beginning (which may mean refreshing your memory at first, if you already know the basics). If you make sure that you fully understand each move or hint before you continue, you will quickly discover how easy it is to master the game. But don't forget that chess is about war and it can be extremely vicious – especially against a player who shows no mercy. You need to be skilful and ruthless, while considering your moves. Despite this (or perhaps because of it), chess remains one of the greatest and most satisfying boardgames in the world.

Setting up the Board

Chess is a war game played out over sixty-four squares between two players who control White and Black armies which both consist of sixteen chessmen. The players move in turns but White always has the opening move in a game. In tournament chess, if you are White you are considered to have an advantage (in that you initially have more influence over the game).

At the beginning of each game, the chessboard is set up in the starting position (RIGHT), with the pieces (this usually refers specifically to the kings, queens, rooks, bishops and knights) on their own squares on opposite sides of the board, and a row of pawns in front of them. The chessmen move across the board in different ways, and some are worth more than others (this is explained on the following pages).

Both queens initially stand in the centre of the board on their own colours. In other words, the Black queen is on a black (or dark-coloured) square and the White queen is on a white (or pale-coloured) square. Next to each queen (going from the centre outwards) are a bishop, a knight and a rook. The king starts out on the other central square (next to its queen) and also has a bishop, knight and rook to its side (to the right, if you are White, or to the left, if you are Black).

The chessboard should always be placed so that there is a white (or pale-coloured) square in the right-hand corner.

When the game begins and the armies start to advance, at first the pieces move to unoccupied squares. However, later in the game a piece can be moved to a square which has an enemy piece on it. The enemy is then 'captured' and is removed from the board. Unlike in some other board games, you cannot have two pieces (of either colour) occupying the same square at the same time.

NOTE ...
before you start to play, it is wise to make sure that the chessboard is stable, to prevent it from being 'accidentally' knocked by a player whose imminent defeat seems unavoidable.

The King

The object of chess is to capture your enemy's king. If there is a clear winner at the end of the game, the situation will be what is described as 'checkmate' (see page 32). This means that the losing king cannot escape capture and the battle is over. For this reason, the king should be well defended by his army throughout the game and kept far away from the heat of the battle.

The term 'checkmate' derives from the words *shah* and *mat*. In the sixth century AD, chess spread from India to Persia, where the king was known as the *shah*. When the *shah* was trapped it was said to be *mat*, which means 'defeated' or 'helpless'. Most of the chess pieces today retain something of their ancient origins.

The king may move one square in ANY DIRECTION, but it may *not* move to a square which is already occupied by one of its own pieces, or to a square which is adjacent to the enemy king. In addition, the king is also not allowed to move to a square where it is checked – which means being attacked – by an enemy piece (see page 32).

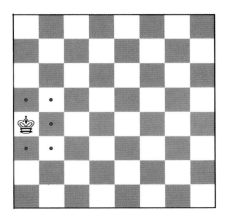

The king may move to any of the indicated squares.

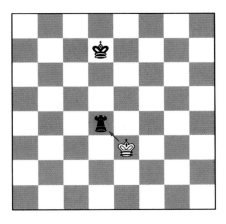

White can move here to capture the rook.

This is how the king appears on the diagrams in this book. You may see slightly different symbols in other chess publications, but the king is always easy to identify because it has a cross on the top. Another chess convention is that White's army usually occupies the bottom half of chess diagrams.

The Rook

The rook was originally a chariot (*rukh* means 'chariot' in Arabic), but when the game spread to Europe in the Middle Ages, the piece became a tower or castle, reflecting the kind of siege warfare that frequently occurred in those days. Sometimes the piece is still referred to as a castle, although it is more correctly known as a rook.

The rook may move HORIZONTALLY or VERTICALLY any number of squares, so long as there is no piece blocking its path.

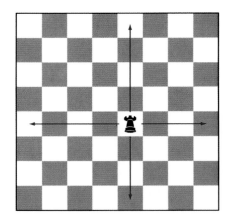

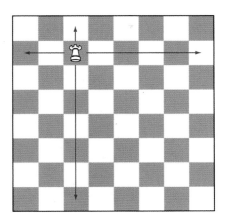

The rook may move to any of the squares along the arrows.

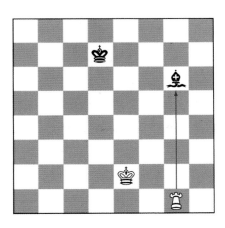

White's best move here would be to capture the bishop.

With the exception of the king, each piece has a numerical value. The rook is worth 5 points. The relative values of pieces can help you to decide, among other things, whether or not it is a good idea to capture a piece that is defended. However, these values are only for guidance. Remember that you cannot win on points; the aim is to achieve checkmate.

The Bishop

Each army is blessed with two bishops: one Black and one White bishop run along the black squares, and the other two move along the white ones.

In the original Indian game of *chaturanga*, the piece now called a bishop was actually an elephant, and this survived when the Arabs took up the game. However, elephants meant little to Europeans – the last ones they had seen came over the Alps with Hannibal – so the piece changed in character.

In view of its proximity to the king and queen at the start of the game, the piece was seen as their close adviser. In medieval society this role was usually taken by a church dignitary, and so the elephant was replaced with a bishop. Interestingly, the elephant survives today in more than one country, if not in design then in language. The Spanish word for the piece is *alfil*, which derives directly from the Arabic; and the Russian, *slon*, also means 'elephant'.

The bishop may move DIAGONALLY any number of squares, FORWARDS or BACKWARDS, so long as there is no piece blocking its path.

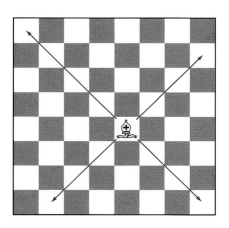

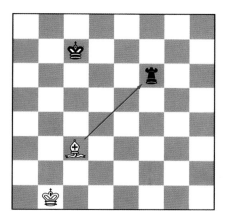

The bishop may capture the rook.

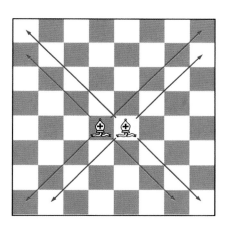

Since the bishops in each army run on opposite colours, they compliment each other perfectly. Commentators often refer to the power of the 'bishop pair' in master games.

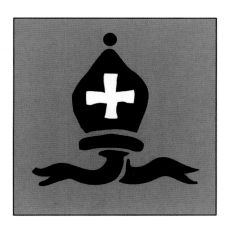

The bishop has a value of 3 points, which means that it is roughly equivalent to a knight (described on page 20). You need to remember this during the game, whenever you are considering exchanging or sacrificing pieces.

The Queen

In the earliest forms of chess in India and Persia, the piece now called the queen was known as a wise man or counsellor (the Persian name *farzin* actually survives in the Russian word for the queen *ferz*). At that time, the piece had feeble powers and could not even move as far as a bishop. It is not clear how this minister transformed itself to a queen, though the simplest and most likely explanation is that the king and queen used to sit side by side in the medieval court, and this was eventually mirrored on the chessboard.

The queen may move any number of squares in any direction – VERTICALLY, HORIZONTALLY or DIAGONALLY – so long as no piece is blocking its path.

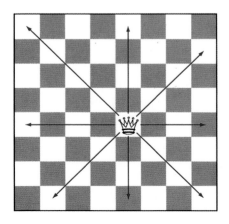

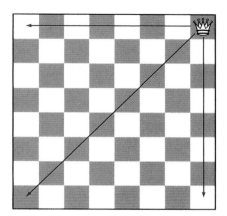

The queen may move to any of the squares along the arrows – provided there is nothing in its way.

The queen can take the bishop.

The queen is the most powerful of all the pieces because it commands the greatest number of squares on an open board. It is given a value of 9 points.

Very often, if you can capture your opponent's queen without losing yours, you should be close to victory.

The Knight

As with the rook and the king, the way in which the knights move around the chessboard has remained the same since the very beginnings of chess in India. When the game came to England in medieval times, however, the piece's name was changed from a horse to a knight, although it is still represented by the animal's head. (Only those unfamiliar with the game incorrectly refer to the piece by its original name.)

The knight either moves two squares horizontally and then one square vertically, or two squares vertically and then one square horizontally. This may sound complicated, but it is quite easy to remember if you think of the move as an 'L' SHAPE which may be inverted, mirrored, and/or rotated.

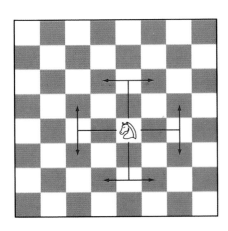

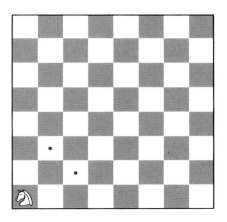

When it is in the centre of the board, a knight is able to move to one of eight squares. If it is stuck in a corner, however, its choice is restricted to only two. This is why it is normally best to keep knights in the middle of the board, where more options are available to them.

A knight has a property peculiar to itself which is that it can jump over a piece in its way. So, for instance, in this diagram, the knight may capture one of Black's pawns.

The knight is worth 3 points, roughly the same as a bishop but not as much as a rook (5 points) or a queen (9 points). To reflect this, bishops and knights are described as minor pieces and queens and rooks as major pieces. With a combined value of 6 points, a knight and a bishop together are usually worth more than a lone rook but not as much as two rooks or just a queen.

The Pawn

Although the pawn can only advance slowly into battle, it would be a despot's ideal foot soldier because, unlike all the other pieces, it is not allowed to retreat. Pawns are often underestimated, especially by those new to the game, because of all the chessmen they are the least powerful. However, as in any fight, if you plan the pawns' formation and always consider their position in conjunction with the other pieces, you will find that they  might allow you to dominate the game. Their value is very difficult to assess because they fulfil so many different functions.

In theory, the pawn may only move one square at a time VERTICALLY up the board. The exceptions to this rule are when a pawn moves at the very beginning of a game and when it is capturing a piece.

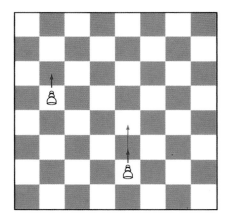

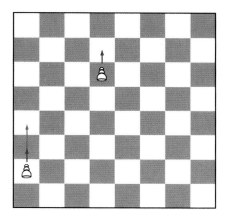

From its starting position the pawn may advance either one or two squares; thereafter it may only move one square at a time.

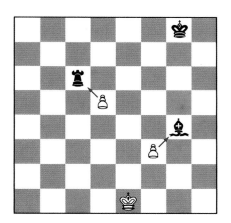

Unlike all the other pieces, pawns capture in a different way to how they normally move, by taking one square DIAGONALLY forwards. Here, for instance, White has a choice between capturing either the bishop or the rook. Pawns can also make a special capturing move known as en passant (see page 40).

The pawn has a value of only 1 point. This means that it is nearly always worth exchanging a pawn for an enemy piece or sacrificing a pawn in order to strengthen your position on the board.

Whenever you see this red arrow, it means that the instructions continue over the page.

There is one further property that the pawn has which makes it unusual. When it reaches the end of the board, it is exchanged for any piece of its own colour: queen, rook, bishop or knight – but not another king. This is known as 'promoting' a pawn. In the vast majority of cases a queen will be chosen, as it is the most powerful piece on the chessboard.

If you still have your original queen (and you are promoting a pawn to a second queen), the new queen is usually represented by a rook turned upside-down. In many tournaments, however, a real queen will probably be used from another chess set.

So, the paradox of the pawn is that while it is the least mobile of all the chess pieces, at the same time it has the potential to transform itself into the most powerful one on the board.

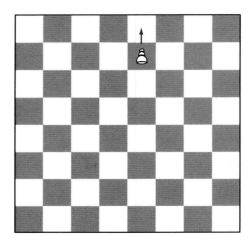

What possible pawn moves can White make in this position? Consider all the options before looking at the diagram below.

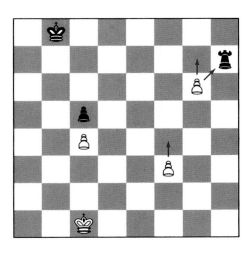

Note how the pawns on the left-hand side of the board are blocked; they cannot move forward nor capture anything. White's best move would definitely be to capture the rook, and then on the next turn it could be pushed to the end of the board and promoted to a queen.

Understanding Notation

Before you start to learn about more complex positions and variations, you need to understand chess notation. This is a type of universal shorthand used to describe moves, and a grasp of this will enable you to read through chess columns in newspapers and look through specialist chess magazines and books.

The most common system, and the one used in this book, is known as 'algebraic notation'. At first glance, the lists of moves may look like indecipherable hieroglyphics, but they are actually very easy to understand. All that is involved is identifying the squares on the board, rather like on a grid used when reading a map or playing the game of battleships. Each diagram has letters along the bottom and numbers up the side.

The letters along the bottom of the board are used to identify the 'files' (the rows of squares going vertically up the board). The numbers identify the 'ranks' (the rows of squares going horizontally across the board). Thus every square can be described by the combination of a letter and a number. For instance, the square in the bottom left-hand corner of the board is a1.

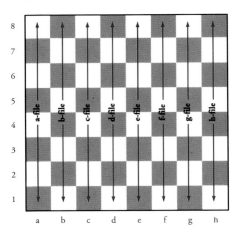

REMEMBER ...
squares are always named with a lower-case letter, then a number. When a move is recorded, the piece that is being moved is written first, followed by the square that it is going to (not the square it has come from).

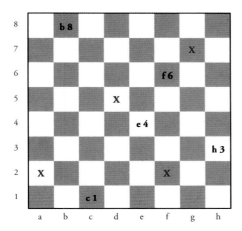

Some of the squares in this diagram have been identified with the correct notation. To make sure that you have understood the system, write down the notation for the squares marked 'X'.

ANSWERS ON PAGE 96

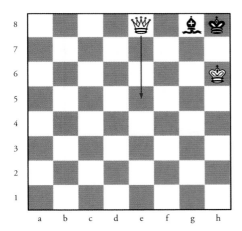

Take a look at this position:

White can give checkmate in one move by playing the queen to the e5 square. This would be recorded as:

1   Qe5 mate.

The '1' at the beginning is the number of the move after the diagram. The 'Q' stands for queen; 'e5' is the square the queen moves to; 'mate' is simply a common abbreviation for 'checkmate'. Sometimes the symbol # is used to represent checkmate, but it is rare.

To save space, the piece that is being moved is never written out in full but is represented by an initial.

The exception is that *a pawn is not given a letter*, only the square that a pawn moves to is noted.

The pieces are recorded as follows:
  K   king
  Q   queen
  R   rook
  B   bishop
  N   knight
To prevent possible confusion with the king, the knight is represented by the phonetic 'N' (or sometimes as Kt). Capitals are always used for the pieces and lower-case letters for the squares.

Beginning with the next diagram, have a go at playing through the moves that follow to help to familiarize yourself with notation. The symbol '+' means 'check'.

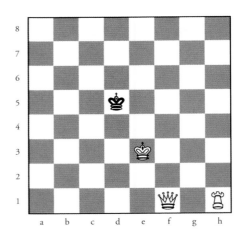

WHITE   BLACK

1 Qb5+ Ke6

2 Rh6+ Kf7

3 Qd7+ Kf8

4 Rh8 mate.

If you have followed the notation correctly, the pieces on the board should now be in this position (RIGHT).

In general, the moves are given in two columns (with White's moves first) as above. However, you might also see them written like this:

1 Qb5+ Ke6   2 Rh6+ Kf7
3 Qd7+ Kf8   4 Rh8 mate.

Note how the squares are identified in the same way, regardless of whether it is Black's or White's move. Remember that the letters always begin at White's bottom left-hand corner (a) going across to the bottom right corner (h), and the numbers go from the bottom rank (1) to the top one (8).

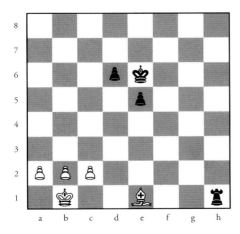

In this position Black is to play; he can give checkmate in one move. Can you see what the move is? It would be recorded as follows:

1 … Rxe1 mate.

Captures are denoted by a lower-case 'x' which always comes after the piece, and before the square. When it is a Black move, and not a White one, three dots appear after the move number and before the letter and number of the destined square.

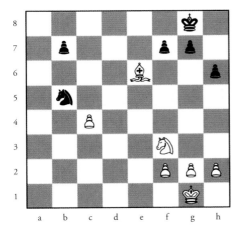

Here (LEFT), if White took Black's knight with the pawn, it would be recorded as follows:

1 cxb5

The file (the vertical row) on which the pawn stands is noted first (the c-file); then the capture sign (x); followed by the square on which the captured piece stands (b5).

If Black were to play here, you would record the pawn capturing White's bishop as

1 … fxe6

Remember that the three dots indicate that it is a Black move.

NOTE …

to keep the notation simple, most of the examples are recorded with a '1', as if they were the first moves of a game. In most cases they are not — this is just a conventional way of recording the first moves in a sequence.

Occasionally, some ambiguity might arise. For instance, in some situations, either of a player's two rooks or knights might be able to move to the destined square.

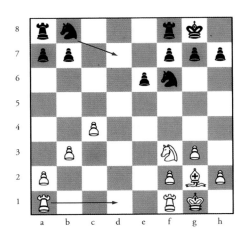

In this position, if White were to play the rook to the centre as indicated by the arrow, how would you record it? Clearly, 1 Rd1 would not be sufficient, because it is unclear as to which rook should move to d1. The ambiguity is solved by writing: 1 Rad1, indicating that it was the rook on the a-file which moved. If the other rook were to move to d1 it would be written 1 Rfd1, because the rook started out on the f-file.

Similarly, when pieces stand on the same file, then the rank should be specified. How would you record the Black knight's move as indicated by the top arrow?

ANSWER ON PAGE 96

ADDITIONAL NOTATION MARKS

Sometimes notation includes additional marks, which are added at the discretion of the commentator.

- If a move has an exclamation mark after it – 1 Nd5! – then the commentator wishes to point out that in his or her opinion it is a good move.

- If there are two exclamation marks – 1 Nd5!! – then it is an outstanding or brilliant move.

- If a move has a question mark after it – 1 Nd5? – then the commentator is pointing out that the move is a mistake.

- If the move has two question marks – 1 Nd5?? – this is a very bad mistake.

To make matters more confusing, these punctuation marks may be combined. For example, 1 Nd5!? usually means that it is an interesting move; and 1 Nd5?! suggests a dubious move. All these assessments are purely subjective.

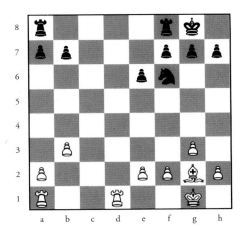

In this position, White is to play and can capture something. Find the move and then put it into chess notation.

ANSWER ON PAGE 96

OTHER TYPES OF NOTATION

Algebraic has superseded other forms of notation because it is clear and simple. However, you might come across two other forms of notation in chess books, magazines or newspapers, so it is useful to know about them. 'Long algebraic' or 'full algebraic' notation is exactly the same as the normal algebraic used in this book, except that the square from which the piece moves is mentioned in addition to the square that it moves to. For instance, if on the sixth move White's knight were to go from d5 to capture a piece on f6, in long algebraic this would be written as 6 Nd5xf6.

'Descriptive' notation is slightly more complicated and, though once popular in the UK and USA, is rarely used today. The ranks are numbered 1 to 8 as with algebraic, and each file is given the name of the piece which was originally placed there at the start of the game. So for instance the a-file in algebraic is the queen's rook file in descriptive notation; the b-file is the queen's knight file, and so on. Each square is thus given a name. So for instance 'e4' in algebraic equals 'king 4' or rather 'K4' in descriptive. If a piece moved there, for instance the pawn on the first move, it would be recorded as 1 P-K4. This is slightly convoluted, but essentially the same as algebraic up to this point. The confusing aspect of this system is that Black numbers the ranks from his own end, not from the same end as White. So, for instance, the square a8 in algebraic would be recorded in descriptive notation as R8 (rook 8) for White, but R1 (rook 1) for Black.

Check and Checkmate

Now you know how all the pieces move and capture, it is time to see how to play the game, remembering that the aim is to trap the enemy king and deliver checkmate. When the king is directly attacked by a piece, it is said to be in CHECK. Some players like to announce 'check' when playing their move, but it is not necessary to do so. In fact, sometimes it may be said more for psychological effect than anything else. In top-level chess it is hardly ever announced and, in fact, might even be considered rude by some players.

Don't panic if you find yourself in check – it is usually just a temporary inconvenience. It is most unlikely that your well-thought-out plans will ever run smoothly; if they do, it probably means that you have failed to appreciate what your opponent is planning. In chess – as in life – you will have to adjust your plans according to the situation you find yourself in. Remember that, if the enemy does put you in check, you *have no option;* you *must* move out of check *immediately.*

The White queen attacks, or rather checks, Black's king. The king *must* now move out of check. Here it has two possible moves.

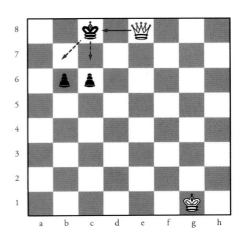

The position has been changed slightly. The White queen once again checks Black's king, but this time the king is trapped: if it moves to the side (either way) it would still be checked (attacked) by White's queen. As the king cannot escape from check, this position is CHECKMATE, so Black loses the game.

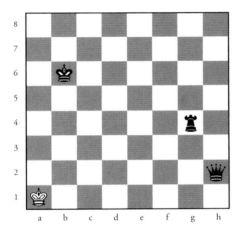

White has just a lone king and it is trapped on the back-rank. Black, with an extra queen and rook, ought to be able to finish off the game fairly rapidly. There are many ways for Black to check the king, but there is also a way to deliver CHECKMATE in one move. See if you can spot it before looking at the next diagram.

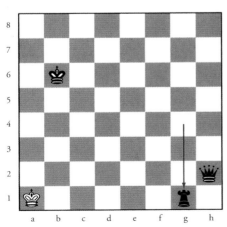

The answer is that the rook moves down to attack the king. White has no way to get out of check (if the king tried to move to a2 or b2, it would be checked by the queen, and at b1 it will still be checked by the rook). So White is CHECKMATED and thus loses the game.

These pages show four more positions where it is possible to deliver checkmate in one move. See if you can spot them. Write down all the answers in notation before you check the solutions.

(a) White to play and checkmate in one move.

ANSWER ON PAGE 36

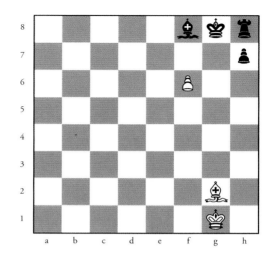

(b) Black to play and checkmate in one move.

ANSWER ON PAGE 36

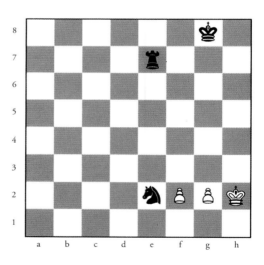

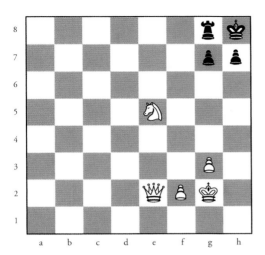

(c) White to play and checkmate in one move.

ANSWER ON PAGE 37

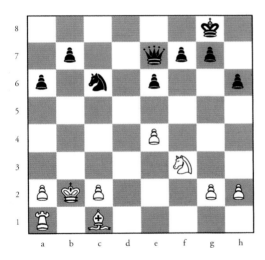

(d) Black to play and checkmate in one move.

ANSWER ON PAGE 37

(a)   White's bishop puts
the king in check; the
king cannot move to the
squares occupied by the
bishop, rook and pawn,
and the other squares are
covered by the pawn and
the bishop. Thus this
position is checkmate. It
would be recorded as :

1   Bd5 mate.

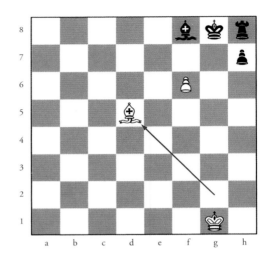

(b)   Black's rook attacks
the king; its flight squares
on the g-file are covered
by its own pawn, and
Black's knight on e2.
The position is
checkmate. Black's move
would be recorded as:

1   ... Rh7 mate.

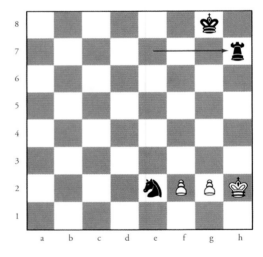

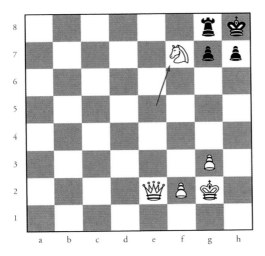

(c)   White's knight checks the king. The king is smothered by its own pieces so this position is checkmate. The move would be recorded as:

1   Nf7 mate.

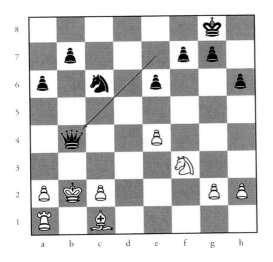

(d)   The Black queen delivers checkmate. It would be recorded as:

1   … Qb4 mate.

Special Moves

Two exceptional moves – castling and en passant – were
introduced in the 16th century to speed up the game.

CASTLING

Castling is a useful and extraordinary coup, which allows you to move your
king and a rook at the same time. When it became part of the game, castling
had a revolutionary effect because it makes it possible to initiate a deadly
attack, from a sound basis, within just a few moves of the start. The term
'castling' comes from the alternative (but seldom used) name for the rook.

You can castle in one of two
ways. Here, the king moves
two squares towards the rook,
and the rook leaps over, and
next to it. On this side of the
board it is known as 'castling
short', or castling king's side.
The move is recorded as 0-0.

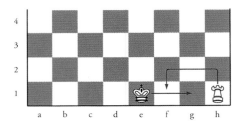

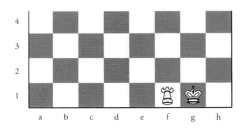

KING'S SIDE AND QUEEN'S SIDE

If you are White, the right-hand
side of the board as you play is your
king's side and the left-hand side is
your queen's side (it's the other way
around for Black). This is easy to
remember if you think of where
the kings and queens stand at the
beginning of the game.

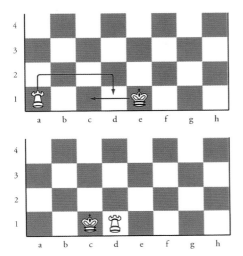

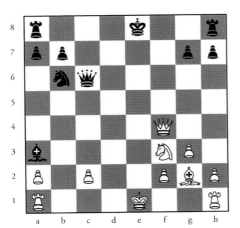

It is also possible to castle queen's side on the other side of the board. Again, the king moves two squares towards the rook, and the rook leaps over and next to it. This is recorded as 0-0-0.

Castling is extremely important. In the vast majority of master games, both players castle. This is because the centre of the board is where the main struggle will be taking place (if you control the centre you dominate the board). It makes sense to move the king to safety at the side of the board, and to bring the rook into the middle, from where it can attack more easily.

If it were White to move in this position (BOTTOM), he could castle on the king's side; but it would *not* be possible to castle queen's side because the king would land in check (from the bishop on a3). If it were Black to play, he would *not* be able to castle king's side: the king cannot move through the line of attack from the queen on f4. However, castling queen's side would be possible.

WHEN YOU CANNOT CASTLE
- If there is a piece standing between the king and the rook.
- If the king or rook has already been moved.
- If the king is in check.
- If the king has to cross a square guarded by an enemy piece.
- If your king will be in check after castling.

REMEMBER ...
castling is one of the most valuable and useful moves of the game.

En Passant

The en passant rule is probably a hangover from the original game of chess, when pawns progressed more slowly and only moved one square from the start. It prevents players from getting away with advancing a pawn two squares every time.

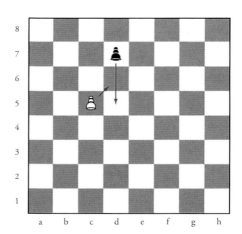

Imagine you were playing White (TOP RIGHT) and the Black pawn moved up two squares next to your pawn. You may then, if you so wish, capture the pawn *as if it had only moved one square* i.e. you take the enemy pawn and move your pawn diagonally behind it. However, this option is only available on the very next move; you can't suddenly think five moves later, 'Now I'll take that pawn!'.

The next position (MIDDLE) illustrates how useful it can be to capture en passant.

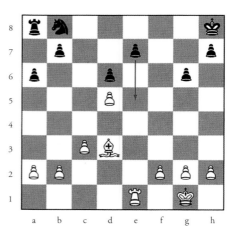

White has just moved the rook to e1, threatening the pawn on e7. There is no way to defend the pawn, though it looks as though he might save himself by playing:

1 ... e5

But White may capture en passant (RIGHT). This would be written: 2 dxe6 e.p.

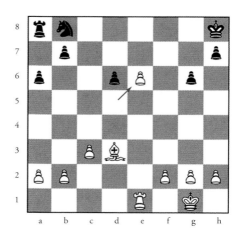

How to Open the Game

Now that you have learned about checkmating and the special moves, it is time to begin the game. If you keep the following aims in mind during the opening phase, you cannot go (too far) wrong.

- CONTROL THE CENTRE.
- DEVELOP YOUR PIECES.
- GET CASTLED AS QUICKLY AS POSSIBLE.

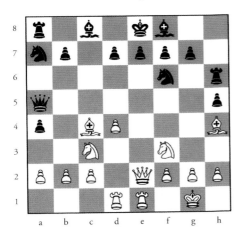

Here, just a few moves into the game, White, guided by the above aims, has built up a dominating position. Black has flouted all three and is therefore looking much weaker.

White has, quite sensibly, castled so his king is tucked away at the side of the board, far from the action in the centre and well protected by a row of pawns. The rest of White's pieces have been brought out to strong positions: the knights are in the centre of the board, well placed to join in an attack; the rooks are also in the centre bearing down on Black's king, as is the queen.

Black, on the other hand, is grovelling around the edges of the board, seemingly afraid to make contact with his opponent. The king is stuck in the middle; the bishops cannot move at all as they are still blocked in by pawns; the pawns at the side, half-way up the board, have no relevance to the struggle; the rook should not have been developed on the flank – if it did emerge it would be very vulnerable to attack (compare this with White's beautifully positioned rooks: they are effectively posted yet are quite safe from attack). To sum up the position, Black is in deep trouble.

Let's return to the starting position and consider the ways in which Black could have avoided such a fate.

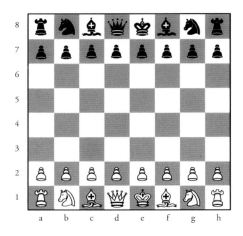

Chess is, essentially, a war game. Just as it would make little sense for a general to leave half of his army behind in the barracks, on the chess board it tends to be most unwise to leave your pieces on their starting squares for too long: the battle could be over before they have a chance to fight (indeed, it is likely to be over very quickly if they don't get involved). Therefore, it is vital to bring *all* your pieces out, as quickly as possible. If we look at the starting position, you will see that both sides may only move their pawns and knights. In order to develop your pieces (this means 'bring them out' in chess jargon), at least two of the pawns will have to be moved forward. Remembering all the hints and moves you have learnt so far, which of these moves do you think it is best for White to begin with?

(a)   1 a4   (b)   1 e4   (c)   1 f3.

The best move is definitely 1 e4 : it releases the bishop on f1, as well as the queen, and stakes a claim in the centre of the board.

This is one of the most popular opening moves, and is the one that I always play, but there are other equally good ways to start the game, most notably 1 d4. This also releases the queen and a bishop, and occupies one of the central squares. In general, pawns should only be moved in the opening for one of two reasons: either to clear the way for pieces to come out, or to win territory in the centre of the board.

Now follow these moves:

1 d4 d5   2 b4 Nf6   3 c3 Bg4   4 g3 e6   5 a4 Bd6   6 h4 0-0   7 a5.

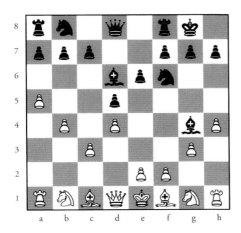

Black has already brought his king to safety by castling, and has developed two bishops and a knight on strong central squares. Only two pawn moves have been made: 1 ... d5 released the bishop on c8 and gained space in the centre, and the other pawn move (4 ... e6) allowed the other bishop to be moved out, which in turn gave Black the chance to castle.

One of White's pawn moves was good (1 d4), but it certainly wasn't necessary to make the other six. Time is a vital factor in the opening. Here, Black is essentially five moves ahead of White – enough to have me looking for the kill already. A good way to start would be to play 7 ... e5, opening up the centre; if White captures, I would take back with the bishop (an equal exchange, with neither side gaining or losing) then I would be ready to move my rook into the middle of the board to e8, whence it casts a shadow over the enemy king. White's undeveloped pieces will be mere spectators at the coming rout.

Let's return to the second move of the sequence above.

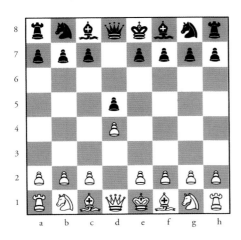

White's first move was good, but what followed only wasted precious time.

Instead of 2 b4, which did not serve the cause of any of our three opening principles, what would you play instead? Given a choice between the following moves, which do you think is White's best alternative?

(a)   2 Na3
(b)   2 Bf4
(c)   2 a4.

Let's consider the possible moves in turn.

2 a4 would not be good. The pawn move does not contribute to the struggle for the centre; and if you thought it might be a good idea to develop the rook via a3, think again. Many beginners do this and it is a big mistake: the rook is a valuable piece (remember it is worth 5 points), and if it gets attacked by a knight or a bishop (both worth only 3 points), it will have to move. In the opening phase, as all the pieces are on the board, this is very likely to happen. Precious time would be lost, and that could prove fatal. In general, it is better to develop knights and bishops before the rooks and the queen.

2 Na3. A knight is brought out but, unfortunately, not to a very good square. It is always much better for a knight to be placed in the centre than at the side of the board where it has few options.

2 Bf4 is definitely the best option: the bishop is developed to a square where it exerts strong influence over the centre.

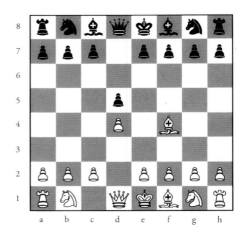

However, this is certainly not the only good move that White has in this position. 2 Nf3 is, naturally, very sensible; and 2 c4 is interesting. 2 c4 is known as the Queen's Gambit. If Black takes the pawn, 2 ... dxc4, then White may play 3 e4, with an imposing pawn centre. There is also a good chance that the pawn on c4 will be recovered by the bishop on f1.

GAMBITS

A gambit is the name given to the sacrifice of a pawn, or occasionally a piece, in the opening, in order to gain an advantage in time or position. The word derives from the 16th-century Italian slang *gambitare* meaning 'to trip someone up' (*gamba* means 'leg'); so an opening which invites a future trap is known as a gambit.

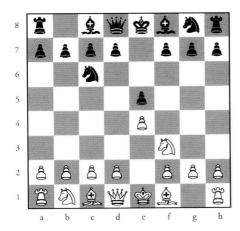

If you open the game with 1 e4, you will find that many of your opponents will follow suit with 1 ... e5, a strong move, not giving any ground in the centre. A good move then would be 2 Nf3, attacking the e-pawn; this ought to be defended, and there are several ways to do so, but 2 ... Nc6, developing a piece at the same time, is the most sensible.

Players have been arriving at this position for centuries, and still have not come to a definite conclusion as to the best way for White to proceed. 3 d4 is a good move; this is known as the Scotch Game as it became popular after a London-Edinburgh match of 1824. There is a threat to the pawn, so Black should capture: 3 ... exd4 4 Nxd4. White has a slightly greater share of the centre, but both sides are able to develop their pieces quite freely.

The most consistently popular move over the past four centuries has been 3 Bb5. This is known as the Spanish Game or, more traditionally, the Ruy Lopez after its inventor, who was a 16th-century Spanish priest.

The bishop move increases the pressure on Black's centre, and prepares for castling. This opening has been a favourite of mine since I first began

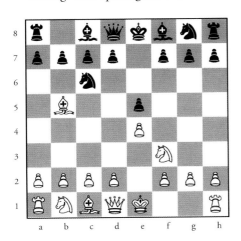

playing chess, usually on the White side, but in the past few years I have defended Black's position as well.

I strongly recommend that you start out with one of these openings, whether playing Black or White: they are classic systems to which the three principles (on page 31) can be applied.

Capturing

So far we have only looked at simple captures involving no complications whatsoever; all you have to do is see them and you instantly know that they are correct. But what would you do in the following position?

It is White to play. The knight may capture either a bishop, a pawn, or a rook. Which piece do you think would be the best one to take?

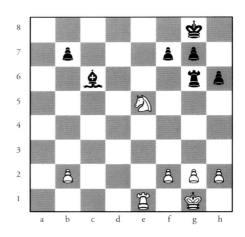

Capturing the pawn would definitely be a mistake: the knight would immediately be recaptured by the king. As the knight is worth 3 points and the pawn only 1 point, this clearly is a bad rate of exchange for White.

Taking the bishop is not a bad option. The knight would be recaptured by either the pawn or the rook, but as the bishop is also worth 3 points this is just an equal exchange; no one loses, no one gains.

Capturing the rook is by far the best move. Even though White loses the knight in return, this is a good trade: remember, the knight is worth 3 points, but the rook is worth 5. In other words, White comes out of this exchange having gained 2 points. You can see how the values of the pieces help to determine whether a capture or an exchange of pieces is good or bad.

REMEMBER ...
the pieces are valued as follows:
    Queen   9 points
    Rook   5 points
    Knight   3 points
    Bishop   3 points
    Pawn   1 point
The king, of course, is priceless.

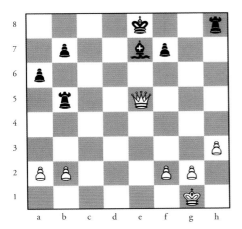

In the following positions, the player to move has a choice of captures. Bearing in mind the relative values of the pieces, decide which is best.

Which piece, if any, should White capture here?

ANSWER ON PAGE 96

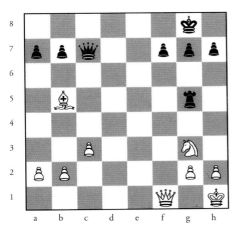

Here should Black:
(a) capture the bishop;
(b) capture the knight;
(c) do something else?

ANSWER ON PAGE 96

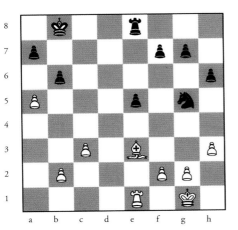

White has a choice of captures; which is best?

ANSWER ON PAGE 96

Simple Checkmates

Assuming that you have managed to capture most of your opponent's pieces, you need to know what to do next, so that you can win the game. Remember that your ultimate aim is to reach checkmate; you can't win a game on points.

It's no use randomly checking your opponent's king, hoping that a mate will turn up. True, there is something in the words of one great master, 'When I give check I am afraid of no one!', just as there is in the words of another, 'Do not give check unless you take something with it!'. But these aphorisms do not help very much. You need to think carefully before you put your opponent in check because you might, in fact, unwittingly be helping the king to run to safety by so doing.

The easiest way to finish off your opponent is to head for one of the basic checkmating positions. Learning these, and mastering the techniques needed to get to them, will be a great help.

Checkmating is easiest when you still have two rooks, or your queen, on the board.

CHECKMATING WITH TWO ROOKS

This is the basic mating pattern to aim for. The king is neatly trapped on the back-rank by one rook, while the other delivers the fatal blow. In order for White to checkmate with just two lone rooks, Black's king must be on the back-rank. So if the king is in the middle of the board, you need to drive it back.

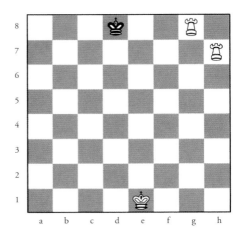

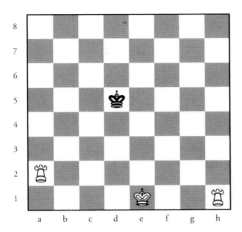

The simplest way is to roll
back the king, gradually using
the rooks to cut off any
possible escape path:

1 Rh4

Black's king can no longer
cross the 4th-rank.

1 ... Ke5

2 Ra5+

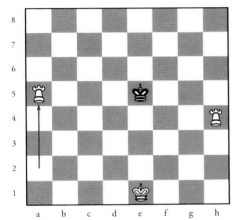

One rook prevents the king
moving back up the board,
and the other actually forces it
backwards by giving check.

2 ... Kf6

3 Rh6+ Kg7

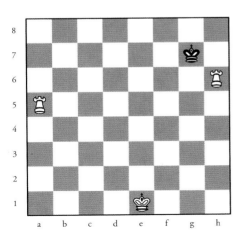

Here, there is a problem,
however. To continue to
make progress, White must
move: 4 Rb6. By switching
sides, White once again has
room to continue the 'rolling'
process. Notice how Black's
king is kept 'cut off': it cannot
cross the 6th-rank while the
rook remains there, because it
would be moving into check.
4 ... Kf7   5 Ra7+
5 ... Ke8   6 Rb8 mate.

The mating pattern shown on page 48 has been reached. This mating technique with two rooks is known as the 'lawn-mower mate': just as no blade of grass is left uncut when a lawn is mown to perfection, so the rooks methodically cover every single square on the board, forcing the king to retreat.

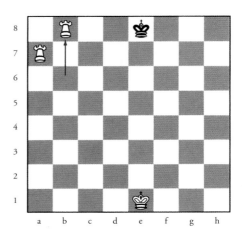

It really is worth rehearsing this technique until you feel completely confident. Find a partner to practise with, or perhaps use your chess computer if you have one. Once you have grasped this, then checkmating with a queen and rook against a king will present no difficulties at all. You use exactly the same technique.

CHECKMATING WITH A LONE QUEEN

Checkmating with a king and queen against a king is a little more difficult. There are two kinds of mating patterns to aim for.

Here, the king cannot take the queen as it would then be on an adjacent square to White's king (which is illegal!); thus the position is checkmate. Just as with the two rooks, Black's king must be forced on to the back-rank in order to give checkmate.

This is the second typical mating pattern. You'll notice that with both these mates, *the queen needs the support of the king.*

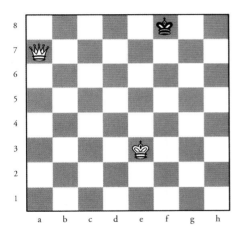

If the king is trapped on the back-rank as here, then checkmating is very simple indeed. White just marches the king up the board:

1 Ke4   Ke8

2 Ke5   Kd8

3 Kd6   Ke8

4. Qe7   mate.

While White's queen remains on the 7th-rank, the Black king cannot move off the back-rank because it would be putting itself into check. Note that if, instead of bringing the king up the board, White had given check with the queen, he would merely have let the king escape.

Here, Black's king is in the centre of the board, so must be driven to the side before it can be checkmated. The technique for doing this is, in principle, similar to that for two rooks: the king's freedom of movement needs to be restricted gradually.

1   Qc4

Black's king is confined within the borders of the box made by White's queen.

1   ... Kf5

2   Qd4

The box grows smaller (RIGHT).

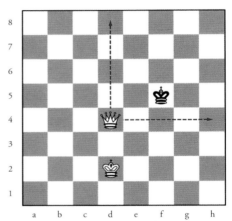

2   ... Ke6

3   Qc5 Kf6

4   Qd5

By stealth, rather than force, Black's king is driven backwards.

4   ... Ke7

5   Qc6

White is getting closer to the ultimate aim of forcing the king to the back-rank.

5   ... Kf7

6   Qd6

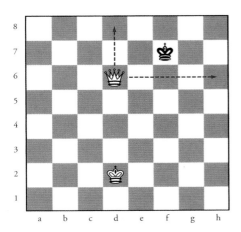

There is no escape for the king.

6   ... Kg7

7   Qe6   Kh8

8   Qe7

So long as White's queen remains here on e7, then Black's king is restricted to just two squares. Now it's a very simple matter just to bring the king up, as in the previous example.

8   ... Kg8

9   Ke3   Kh8

10   Kf4   Kg8

11   Kg5   Kh8

12   Kg6   Kg8

Now White has a choice between 13 Qd8 mate; 13 Qe8 mate or ...

13   Qg7 mate.

Notice how not one check was given throughout the whole of this sequence. The most important thing was to restrict Black's king, which has been successfully achieved.

There is one great danger to
be aware of in this kind of
ending.

Let's go back to White's
8th move (Qe7). You might
think that it would be even
stronger to play:

8 Qf7

In fact, this would end in disaster. Wherever Black's king moves to, it will be
putting itself into check. However, this does not mean that Black is
checkmated. True, Black's king has no legal move, but it is *not in check*. This
situation is known as STALEMATE, and the game would be declared drawn.

Note that just because the
king cannot move, it doesn't
necessarily mean that it is
stalemate. For instance, here
it is Black to play. Would you
say that this is stalemate?

In fact, it is not. Although the
king cannot move, it is still
possible to play the b-pawn
forward:

1 ... b5

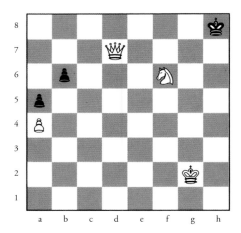

after which White may give
checkmate by playing:

2 Qh7 mate.

Draws

In total, there are six different ways to draw a game of chess; stalemate is only one of them.

By Agreement Between the Two Players

In serious tournament games, this is by far the most common method of making a draw. This is done if there is not enough in the position for either player to go for a win; or a cynic might say that perhaps neither player wishes to risk losing.

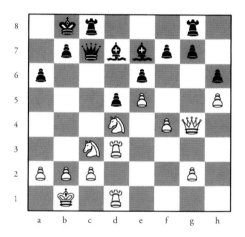

Three-fold Repetition

If exactly the same position is reached on the board on three different occasions, then a player may claim a draw.

This was the conclusion to a game between Mikhail Tal and Mikhail Botvinnik from their 1961 World Championship match:

1 Qe2   Qb6
2 Qg4   Qc7
3 Qe2   Qb6
4 Qg4   Qc7...

and, having repeated the position the third time, the game was declared drawn. Of course, either side could have deviated from the position, but declined to do so (clearly both players were satisfied with a draw).

Insufficient Mating Material

If neither side has sufficient pieces left on the board to checkmate, then the game is drawn. For instance, it is *impossible* to force checkmate with:
- King and bishop against king.
- King and knight against king.
- King and two knights against king.

However, you *can* win with just a lone pawn – because you might well be able to steer it to the other side of the board and promote it to a queen. Mating with just a king and a rook is also possible (see page 84).

Perpetual Check

White's plight looks desperate. Black threatens to move the queen down one square to g2 giving checkmate, and there is no way to prevent it. However, counter-attacking is possible.

1 Qh5+ Kg7
2 Qg5+ Kh8
3 Qh6+ Kg8
4 Qg5+ ... and so on.

Black's king has not been checkmated, but it cannot escape the barrage of checks. The game is then drawn by PERPETUAL CHECK.

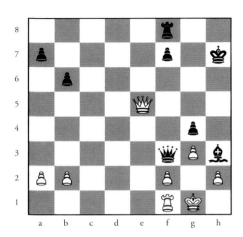

The Fifty Move Rule

If a piece is not captured or a pawn is not moved for fifty moves, then the game may be declared drawn. The instances of this happening are extremely rare, but you should know about it.

Stalemate

The possibility of stalemate usually arises when one side has an overwhelming superiority of forces and is trying to finish off the enemy.

White, wanting to trap Black's king on the back-rank, has just moved the queen up to the e7 square. This is too close. Black's king now has no legal moves but, as it is not in check, the result is stalemate, *not* checkmate.

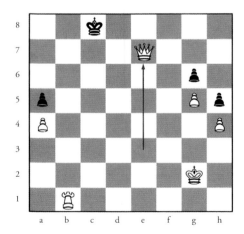

Defending Against an Attack

You have already learned a little about capturing other pieces, but if the reverse happens and one of your pieces is attacked, what should you do? Basically, there are four ways that you can respond when one of your pieces is threatened. In the example (BELOW), White's queen is attacking Black's bishop. Let's consider the four different options available to Black.

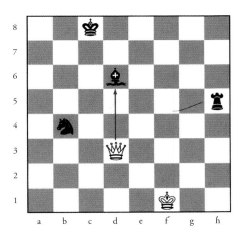

MOVE THE PIECE AWAY
The bishop could move to a number of squares: c5, e7, c7 and so on.

DEFEND THE PIECE
The bishop could either be defended by the king: 1 … Kc7 or 1 … Kd7; or by the rook: 1 … Rh6. Although the queen could still take the bishop, it would immediately be recaptured – with profit for Black.

BLOCKING THE ATTACK
A piece could block the queen's path. For instance:

1 … Nd5   *or*   1 … Rd5.

Again, White would lose material if he decided to capture whichever piece moves to d5.

CAPTURE THE ATTACKER
As you have no doubt spotted by now, the best way of dealing with the threat to the bishop is to retaliate by taking the queen – an easy solution:

1 … Nxd3

REMEMBER …
if one of your pieces is
attacked either:
- • Move
- • Defend
- • Block *or*
- • Capture.

Black's knight attacks the
d-pawn. How can White, to
play, deal with the threat?

ANSWER ON PAGE 96

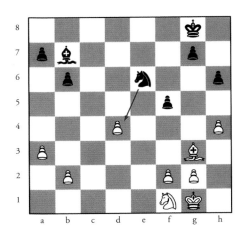

White has just moved the
rook to the h-file attacking
the knight. How would you
deal with the threat?

ANSWER ON PAGE 96

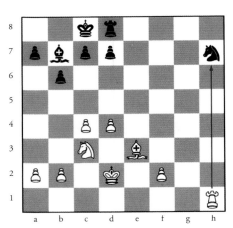

White's bishop on a4 attacks
the knight. There is more
than one way of dealing with
the threat. Find two ways in
which Black, to play, can save
the knight.

ANSWER ON PAGE 96

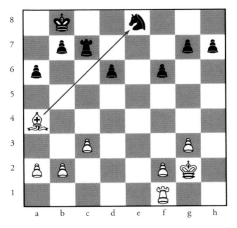

Getting Out of Check

If your king is in check, your next move *must* be to get out of check. When looking for the best way to do this, you can apply similar methods to those used when another piece is threatened. Although the king cannot be defended in the same way as an attacked piece, 'move, block and capture' still apply.

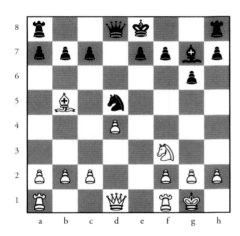

White's bishop has just given check. Capturing the piece is not possible, so would you:

• Block the check
   or
• Move the king?

> NOTE ...
> unfortunately, you cannot castle out of check.

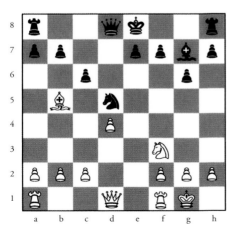

Blocking the check would be the most sensible move (though not with your queen). After 1 ... c6, the bishop is actually attacked and therefore has to waste a move retreating.

Moving the king would not be such a good idea as castling would then be impossible. While the king crawls to the side of the board, the rook in the corner would be stuck out of play.

Scholar's Mate

Although the two opposing armies look far away from each other at the start of the game, you should still be wary of traps right from th word 'go'. There is one in particular, a four-move checkmate knowr as 'Scholar's Mate', which you simply *must* know about. I'm not suggesting that you would be devious enough to try it on your opponent, but someone is bound to try it on you, so it's essential to be prepared. Scholar's Mate goes like this:

1 e4 e5

As you already know, the centre of the board is very important, so these pawn moves make good sense. The opening fits in with the classic principles of occupying the centre.

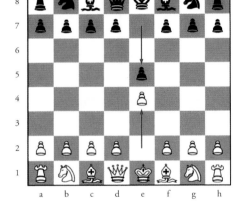

2 Bc4 Bc5

White brings the bishop to a good post in the centre and Black follows suit.

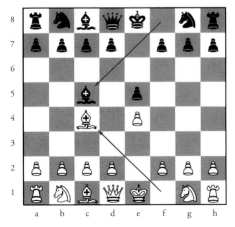

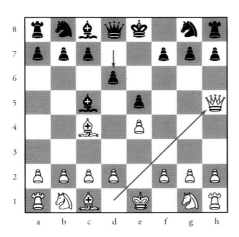

3 Qh5 d6

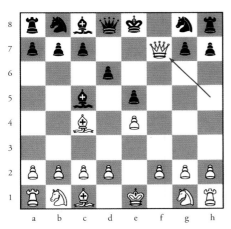

4 Qxf7 mate

The queen comes down to take the pawn and delivers checkmate.

The king cannot take the queen as it is protected by the bishop. This is all very dramatic. Can you see where exactly Black went wrong? Let's return to the position after 3 Qh5.

3 Qh5 is a tricky move. Not only is the checkmate threatened, but Black's e-pawn is attacked as well.

• Remember the four ways of defending against an attack. Black actually has two moves which defend against both threats.
• Capturing isn't possible.
• Moving the pawn is illegal, apart from anything else (the king would put itself into check).

• Blocking is possible, but a very bad idea. If 3 … g6 4 Qxe5+, followed by taking the rook in the corner. (This two-pronged attack is known as a 'fork' – see page 68).

There are, however, two ways in which it is possible to defend both pawns: 3 … Qf6 (which incidentally threatens … Qxf2+); and 3 … Qe7. In both cases, the queen could still capture on f7, but after the exchange of pieces, Black would emerge ahead on points (work it through slowly for yourself if you are unsure).

I think I would play 3 … Qe7, for on the next move I would be able to drive the queen away with 4 … Nf6, gaining valuable time. This shows how going for Scholar's Mate is a gamble: you might be successful with it on a few occasions, but if your opponent has any clue at all about what you are doing, your queen will have to beat an undignified retreat.

Before you go any further, look at the moves of a game between the former world champion Boris Spassky (Black) and a hitherto unknown German named Harald Lieb (White). The game was played in Munich in 1979. (It will be good practice for you with the notation, though if you still find it difficult to follow in your head, play through the moves on your chessboard.)

1 e4   e5
2 Nc3   Nf6
3 Bc4   Nc6
4 d3   Bc5
5 f4   d6
6 Na4   Bxg1
7 Rxg1 Ng4
8 g3   exf4
9 Bxf4 Nxh2 (not a good move)
10 Qh5.

Do the positions of White's queen and bishop look familiar? White threatens both checkmate on f7, and the knight on h2, so Spassky, faced with the loss of a piece, resigned the game. It may be reassuring to see that disasters can befall even great players.

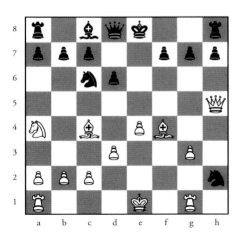

Checkmating Patterns

The queen can be a deadly attacking piece, but in general it is better to wait for a weakening in your opponent's position before throwing it into the fray. The queen is your most valuable piece, so it is important to find it a safe square. The great temptation when you are learning chess is to bring your queen out too soon, but this can be a most unwise move.

It is worth looking at some typical checkmating patterns – particularly with the queen, but with the other pieces too – so that you can spot the right moment to lunge forward. Having glanced at these prototypes, you may be surprised at how frequently the same patterns recur in your games. If you learn to recognize these patterns, you will find that it helps you to finish off your opponent. Some of the positions should already be familiar to you from examples earlier in the book.

Don't try to memorize all the patterns at once, but do experiment by setting up the pieces on your chessboard – this will help to plant them in your subconscious.

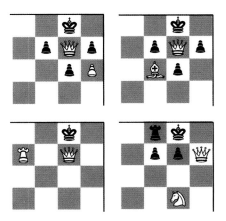

You will notice that in all these examples, Black's king is at the side of the board, in the typical position after castling. This is where you are likely to find the king if you are playing against anyone who takes chess seriously.

As you will see later on, the monarch can suffer a most undesirable fate if left stranded in the middle of the battlefield.

Your king is much more likely to fall prey to an attack if it is exposed, so try to keep a knight or bishop nearby ready to defend.

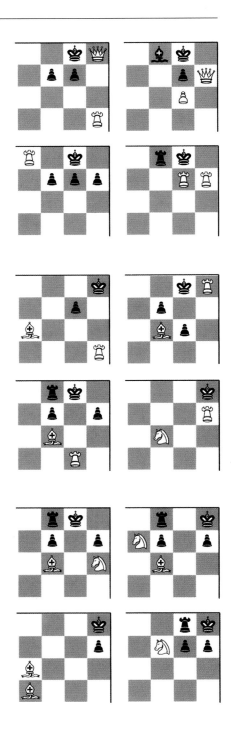

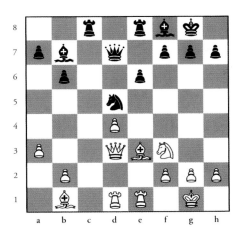

Bearing in mind the prototype checkmating patterns, have a go at solving these positions.

White to play and checkmate in one move.

ANSWER ON PAGE 96

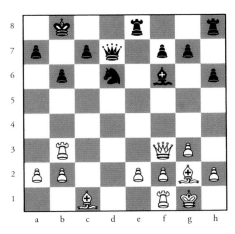

White to play and checkmate in one move.

ANSWER ON PAGE 96

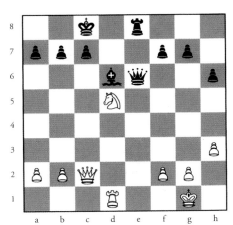

This one is slightly more difficult; Black to play and force checkmate in two moves.

ANSWER ON PAGE 96

White to play and force
checkmate in two moves.

ANSWER ON PAGE 96

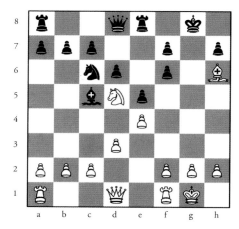

White to play and force
checkmate in two moves.

ANSWER ON PAGE 96

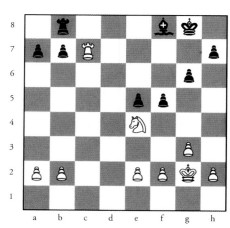

Black to play and checkmate
in two moves.

ANSWER ON PAGE 96

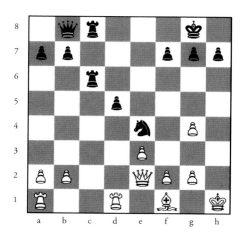

Tactics

A dictionary definition of 'tactics' is 'the science or art of manoeuvering in the presence of the enemy' or 'purposeful procedure'. The second description is perhaps closest to the very specific meaning that 'tactics' (or 'a tactic') has in chess, namely: an attacking device (often a double attack) which results in the win of material or which forces checkmate.

There are many different tactical themes (prepare yourself for some chess jargon): the fork; pin; skewer; discovered attack; discovered check; destroying the guard; breaking communication; trapping; the overworked piece; as well as myriad combinations of these devices. Don't be daunted by this list. Just as with the basic checkmating positions, once you have understood what is involved, with a bit of luck they will drop into your subconscious and you will be able to recall them instantly – and put them to good use – when you see a similar pattern on the board.

Practice is the key; you will find that the more times you see a pattern emerge on the board, the easier it will be to remember them in your future games. It can be quite difficult to visualize each tactic simply by reading the notation, so get out your chessboard and follow through the moves on the following diagrams until you feel totally confident. It doesn't matter if at first you forget the correct terminology for each tactic; the important thing is that you familiarize yourself with the patterns and the moves. However, if you learn the correct names, you will find it helpful if you want to follow the commentary of chess games, perhaps on television, or in chess magazines or newspaper columns.

It will probably help if you concentrate on one tactic at a time, rather than try to tackle them all at once. Rehearse the moves involved until you feel totally confident and ready to move on to the next.

Let's go through each tactic in turn, starting with the fork, which is one of the most satisfying forms of attack.

THE FORK

This is when one piece attacks by moving to a square from which it can capture two or more enemy pieces.

White has just pushed the pawn forward to e5, simultaneously attacking bishop and knight. Whichever piece moves, the other will be captured, so White wins material.

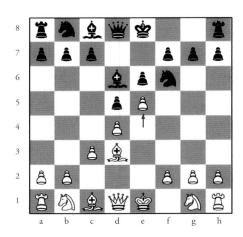

The knight has just moved to f3 giving check, and at the same time attacks White's queen. The king *must* move, so the queen is lost. The knight fork is one of the most lethal (and often unexpected) weapons in the tactical armoury.

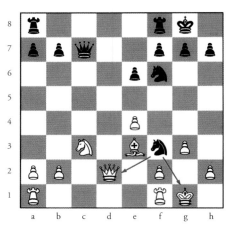

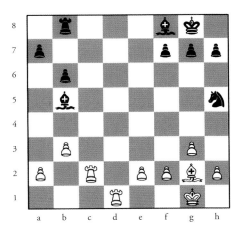

It's not just knights and pawns that are capable of forking other pieces. Take a look at these three positions and see if you can spot the fork in each case.

Here, White is to play.

ANSWER ON PAGE 96

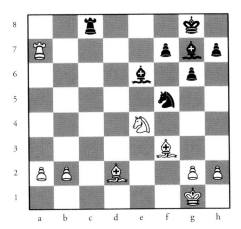

Black to play.

ANSWER ON PAGE 96

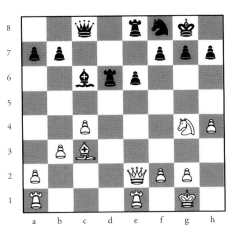

White to play.

ANSWER ON PAGE 96

THE PIN

The pin is an attack against two or more enemy pieces which stand on a straight line (be it file, rank or diagonal).

Black's knight on f6 is pinned to the queen by the bishop on g5. If the knight moves then the bishop takes the queen. White can exploit this immediately by pushing the pawn to e5 attacking the knight; it cannot move so White wins a piece.

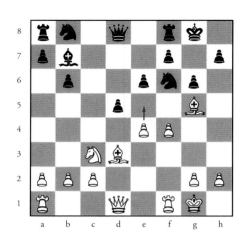

White's rook has just moved from f1, pinning the Black queen to the king. Black must lose the queen – it cannot move because that would put the king into check. Incidentally, this position is a very good illustration of the dangers of leaving your king for too long in the centre of the board, and the advantages of castling early – the rook comes to the centre, in this case with decisive effect.

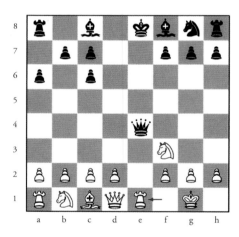

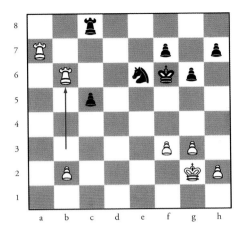

The pin often leads to the win of a piece, as in the first two examples, but sometimes it is just a way of tying up your opponent's pieces for a while, as in this position.

White decides to pin the knight to the king – naturally, not with the idea of playing Rxe6, but simply to reduce the mobility of his opponent's forces.

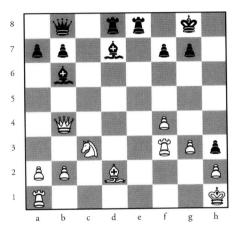

Black, to play, may set up a deadly pin. Can you see how?

ANSWER ON PAGE 96

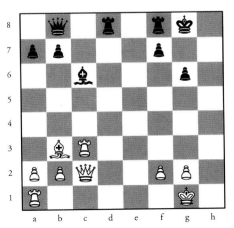

White, to play, may use a pin to initiate a decisive attack against Black's king. Can you see how?

ANSWER ON PAGE 96

The Skewer

A skewer is an attack upon two pieces along the same line, which forces the piece nearest the attacker to move, and which consequently allows the other piece to be taken.

Here, Black's king *must* move out of check, allowing the queen to be taken.

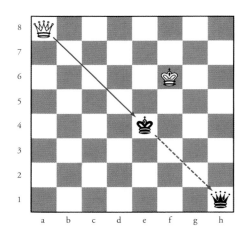

In this position, White must lose his queen, for if it moves, then … Rxf1 is mate.

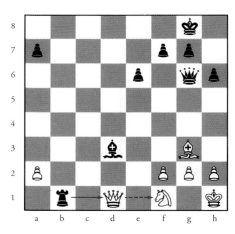

How can Black, to play, set up a skewer, and thus force the win of a piece?

ANSWER ON PAGE 96

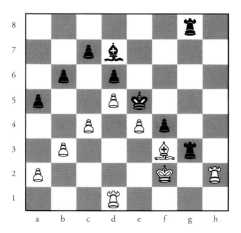

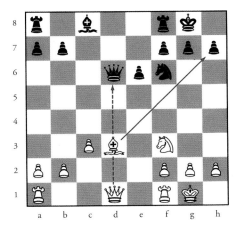

DISCOVERED ATTACK

If one piece moves so that it checks, captures or threatens something, and, at the same time, it unmasks a threat by another piece, this is known as a discovered attack.

In this position, White may play 1 Bxh7+; at first sight it looks suicidal as Black may simply capture, but in fact the point of the move was to unmask the queen on d1, which can then capture Black's queen on d6.

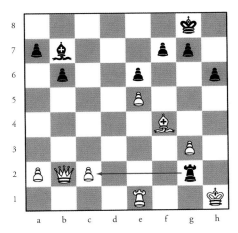

DISCOVERED CHECK

This is very closely related to discovered attack. A piece is moved so that it uncovers a check; while the enemy king is dealing with the check, the piece that moved is wreaking havoc elsewhere on the board.

In this position, Black is actually a whole queen down, but is able to turn the tables by playing ... Rxc2+. The rook move unmasks a check from the bishop on b7, so White's king *must* move out of check, 2 Kg1, and then Black is able to capture the queen on b2: 2 ... Rxb2.

Breaking Communication

Whereas discovered attacks involve opening up a line of attack unexpectedly, breaking communication is about the opposite – closing a line. This would not be a very good idea if, as a result, you end up restricting your own forces. But if you are able to break the harmony in the enemy camp, it can have a devastating effect.

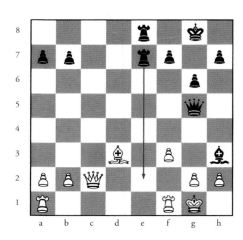

In this position, Black has been angling to play … Qxg2 mate; at the moment, however, White's queen protects g2. Black can get round this by playing 1 … Re2; if White captures, 2 Bxe2, then the communication between the queen and the pawn that it was defending on g2 is broken, so Black may play 2 … Qxg2 mate.

Destroying the Guard

Here, it is White to play. The rook on d1 could take the bishop on d7, but it would immediately be recaptured by the knight on f6. Yet, it is a very simple matter first to capture the knight, 1 Bxf6 gxf6 and then take the bishop, 2 Rxd7, winning a piece. This is called destroying the guard.

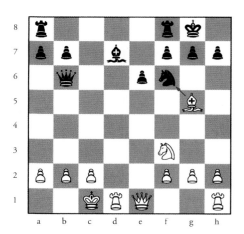

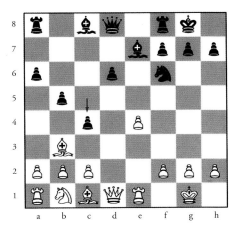

TRAPPING

This tactic – trapping an enemy piece – is a very common way of winning material. Black has just moved the pawn down to c4 attacking the bishop. The bishop's retreat is blocked by its own pawns, and moving to a4 obviously doesn't help, so the piece is lost.

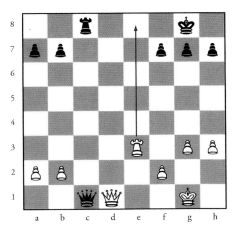

THE OVERLOADED PIECE

When a piece has two duties, perhaps protecting a piece and at the same time guarding an important square, it is said to be overworked or overloaded. Quite often this situation can be exploited to win material.

This is a classic case. Black's rook is protecting the queen on c1 and also guarding against checkmate on the back-rank. White may take advantage of this by playing 1 Re8+; Black's rook is forced to capture, 1 … Rxe8, and now that the rook has relinquished its guard, White can simply take the queen, 2 Qxc1.

In each of the following positions, the player to move can win material by using one of the preceding six tactical motifs. Hinting about where they appear would be giving you too much help. No one stands behind you in a real game telling you what to look for or, at least, they shouldn't. Can you see what the moves should be? In the top diagram, it is Black to play.

ANSWER ON PAGE 96

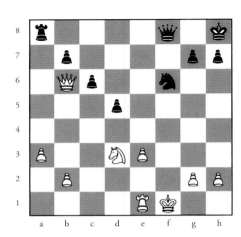

White to play.

ANSWER ON PAGE 96

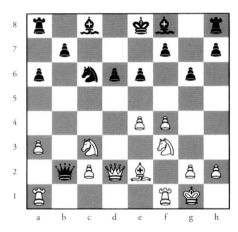

Black to play.

ANSWER ON PAGE 96

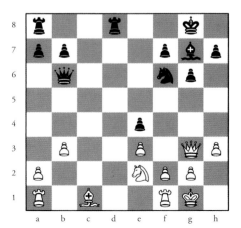

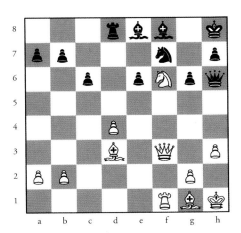

White to play.
ANSWER ON PAGE 96

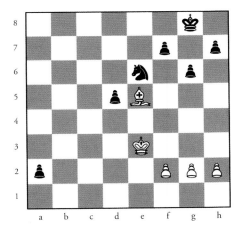

Black to play.
ANSWER ON PAGE 96

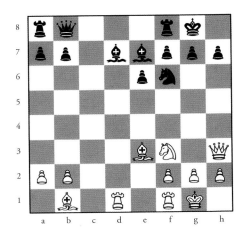

White to play.
ANSWER ON PAGE 96

REMEMBER ...
you are looking for:
• discovered attack;
• discovered check;
• breaking communication;
• destroying the guard;
• overloaded piece; *or*
• trapping.

Playing a Game

It is quite difficult to grasp the significance of tactical ideas when they stand out of context, so let's now look at a complete game. This will also be a useful way of recapping on the three opening principles. The following game is one of my own efforts which I played against Max Fuller at a tournament in London in 1977. It is unlikely that you will be able to follow the game move for move when you next play – unfortunately one's opponents are rarely so co-operative – but you will certainly be able to apply the underlying principles which it demonstrates.

1 e4

This is my favourite opening move.

1 ... c5

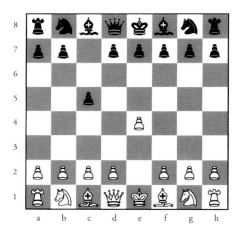

This is known as the Sicilian Defence; it is one of the most popular openings in the world, and a particular favourite of Garry Kasparov.
    Like 1 ... e5 (see page 43), 1 ... c5 also controls an important central square – d4 – but it breaks the symmetry, so is more dynamic.

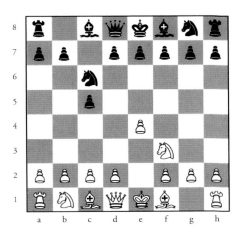

2   Nf3

This brings the knight to a good central square.

2   … Nc6

And Black does the same.

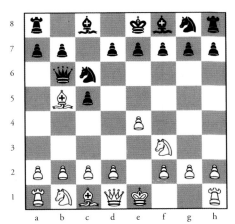

3   Bb5

Now the bishop is developed to an active square and I am preparing to get my king castled as quickly as possible.

3   … Qb6

Studying Scholar's Mate (see page 60) shows how risky it can be to bring out the queen too early. This move is actually the beginning of Black's problems.

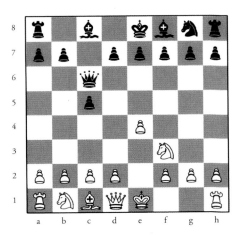

4   Bxc6

The bishop was attacked so something had to be done. Remember that one of the three principles for the opening is to castle as quickly as possible – but not at the expense of losing a piece.

4   … Qxc6

5   0-0 (RIGHT)

If Black now took my e-pawn
it would be suicidal: I could
gain time for developing my
pieces by threatening the queen
and start an attack along the
open e-file. For one pawn this
is a bargain.

5   ... g6

This is a sensible move,
preparing to bring out the bishop.

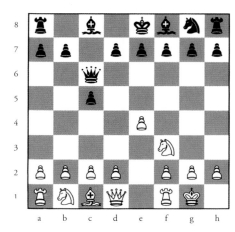

6   Nc3 Bg7   7   d4

I have brought out more pieces than my opponent, so it makes sense to open
up the position in the hope that I can catch his king in the middle of the board.

7   ... d6   8   dxc5 dxc5   9   Bf4

If Black had simply brought out the knight – 9 ... Nf6 – and castled, his
position would be playable; but greed finally got the better of him and he
snapped up a pawn. First, he removes the piece which defends the pawn
(destroying the guard).

9   ... Bxc3   10   bxc3 Qxe4

11   Qc1 (RIGHT)

I am defending the bishop
which was attacked by the
queen.

11   ... Bf5

If Black had played
11 ... Nf6 instead, in an
attempt to castle king's side,
12 Bh6 would have been very
strong, keeping Black's king
trapped in the centre.

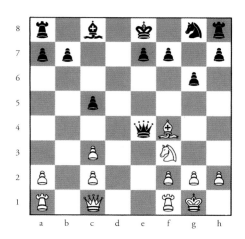

12   Re1 Qa4

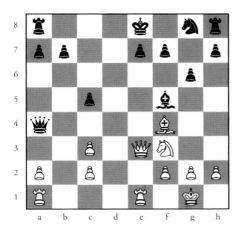

13 Qe3

Black had ideas to bring his king to safety on the queen's side – which this move effectively prevents: if 13 ... 0-0-0 14 Qxc5+ with a strong attack.

Alternatively, if 13 ... Nf6 14 Qxe7 is mate. This is a clear demonstration of how dangerous it is to open up files in front of the king.

13 ... Qc6

14 Ne5 Qc8

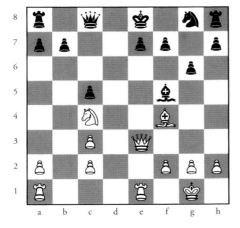

15 Nc4

It is important not to give Black any room to breathe. The knight has come into the attack by gaining time against the queen.

I have a deadly threat in this position: 16 Nd6+, which is a classic example of a knight fork; the king *must* move and then I take the queen. The pawn cannot take the knight as it is pinned to the king by the queen.

15 ... Be6

16 Qe5

Black has only one effective way to defend the rook in the corner. If 16 ... f6   17 Qxe6 wins a piece.

16 ... Nf6

Black is threatening to bring his king to safety by castling, so White must react immediately to prevent this. The move which I played in the game is the most effective way of doing this, but 17 Bh6 was also possible.

17 Nd6+ exd6   18 Qxf6

I have not won any material – this was just an equal exchange – but I have managed to get my queen deep into the heart of my opponent's position. Black may still castle here, but that would have disastrous consequences: 18 ... 0-0 19 Bh6, and there is no way to prevent 20 Qg7 mate. Does this mating pattern look familiar?

18 ... Rg8   19 Bxd6

This threatens a similar mate on e7.

19 ... Qd7

20 Rad1

This defends the bishop and brings my last piece into the attack. I hope you'll forgive me for saying that I like my position very much! Compare my beautifully centralized forces with Black's, effectively split in two while the king remains in the middle of the board.

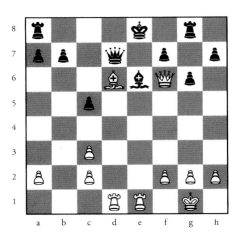

Here my opponent found it all a bit too much and resigned the game. In tournament chess this is quite normal – as we shall see in a moment, Black's position is quite hopeless – but I would not recommend you do this in your games. *Play them all out to the bitter end, to checkmate.* It is amazing how the tables can turn even in seemingly lost situations; besides, your opponent might not know how to finish you off.

    To return to the game, there is actually nothing Black can do to prevent me playing as follows:

21   Bxc5

with a discovered attack against the queen from the rook on d1. The queen must keep covering the e7 square to prevent White's queen checkmating so

21   ... Qc7

is forced, whereupon White may crash through with

22   Rxe6+ fxe6

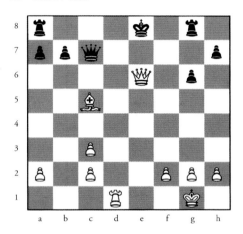

23   Qxe6+, forcing checkmate.

My opponent's big mistake in this game was to pay too little attention to the development of his pieces. Instead of sending his queen on a merry journey around the board, he should have developed his other pieces, and most importantly, brought his king to safety by castling.

REMEMBER THE OPENING PRINCIPLES
• CONTROL THE CENTRE. Use your pawns to carve out territory and follow up with your pieces.
• DEVELOP YOUR PIECES. In general, bring out your knights and bishops first; move your rooks to open files where they are not blocked by pawns; and wait for a good moment before hurling your queen into the attack. If you move it into the thick of the struggle too soon it will only be driven away, so losing valuable time.
• CASTLE AS QUICKLY AS POSSIBLE. The dangers of leaving the king in the centre for too long should be clear by now. On a more positive note, castling brings a rook into the centre of the board where it can play a useful part in the struggle.

The Rook Checkmate

There is one more basic checkmate to consider. You won't have to checkmate with a lone rook very often, but if it should arise, you would feel pretty foolish if you couldn't finish off your opponent. Mastering the techniques involved will also give you a good feel for how the rook moves, which will definitely help when it comes to playing the endgame (see page 88). Play through the following examples a few times until you fully understand the moves involved. After that, practise the ending with a partner, taking turns with the rook, until you both feel confident with the moves.

These are the two mating positions to aim for – one in the corner of the board and the other at the side.

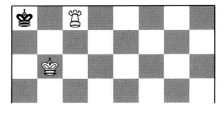

Just as when checkmating with a lone queen, the first objective should be to drive the king to the side of the board. This is done by enclosing the king within a box of squares. (We have used this technique before with the queen, though here it is not quite so easy.) You need to use the king and the rook in close co-operation.

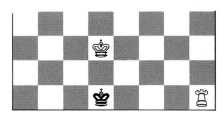

1   Rh5

After this, Black's king cannot step over the fifth rank.

1   ...Ke6

The next stage is to bring the king up to help the rook. Only in this way can Black's king be driven back.

2   Ke3   Kd6

3   Kd4   Ke6

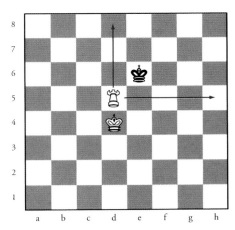

4   Rd5

The rook creates a box, confining the king. Note that checking would not help; restriction is the key.

4   ... Kf6

5   Re5

White seizes the chance to make the box smaller.

5   ... Kf7

6   Kd5

As it is not possible to improve the position of the rook, the king is advanced further.

6   ... Kf6   7   Kd6

Once again, moving the rook would have had little point (it would merely have let Black's king escape), so the king moves again. This is really a waiting move; it has the effect of forcing Black's king backwards

7   ... Kf7   8   Re6

further confining the king.

8   ... Kg7   9   Ke7   Kg8   10   Rg6+ Kh7   11   Kf7

From this position,
Black has only one move:

11 ... Kh8

12 Rh6 mate.

HOW TO FORCE CHECKMATE

The different stages involved in forcing checkmate can be summarized
as follows:

- Confine the enemy king by using the rook.
- Bring up your king to support the rook.
- Use the rook to create a box confining the king. If it is possible to
  make this box smaller, do so.
- If you cannot make the box smaller, move your king (a waiting move
  to force back the enemy king).
- Once the king has been forced to the side of the board, go for one of
  the two checkmating positions you should be aiming for.

By now you ought to be familiar with the technique of using the rook to
create a box. The most difficult part of the process is the waiting move. When
the enemy king is being forced back, remember that you need to play waiting
moves with the king. Often, when the king is on the back-rank, a waiting
move with the rook will force checkmate.

Here, White forces mate by playing a waiting move with the rook:

1   Rf1 Kh8

2   Rf8 mate.

Any rook move down the f-file on the first move would do the trick.

How can White force a quick checkmate from this position?

ANSWER ON PAGE 96

The Endgame

In theory, a game of chess usually consists of three distinct phases. These are the opening, when both armies come out; the middle-game, when the attacks and tactics come into play; and finally (assuming that there is still something remaining on the battlefield) the endgame. It is unlikely that violent attacks will occur during this phase because there are simply too few pieces on the board. Tactics are still important, but they do not dominate as in the middle-game.

So how, then, are you supposed to gain a winning advantage? Very often the best plan is to try to promote one of your pawns into a queen.

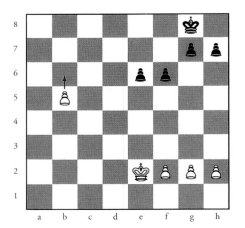

Here White, to play, wins by simply pushing the b-pawn up the board to the 8th-rank and getting a queen.

When a pawn has no enemy pawns either to the side or in front of it, as is the case here, it is said to be 'passed'. Because of their great potential, passed pawns are very valuable – particularly in endings where there are few pieces which can stop them marching down the board.

Black may successfully promote his pawn to a queen in this position. How?

ANSWER ON PAGE 96

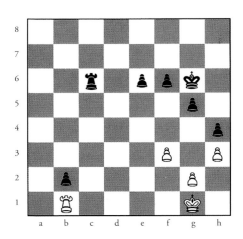

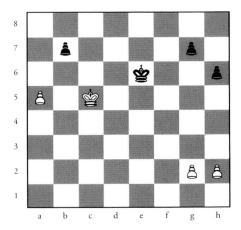

How should White play this position?

White can win by taking Black's b-pawn with his king: 1 Kb6 and 2 Kxb7, followed by queening the a-pawn. Black can do nothing to prevent this.

Although it is vital to keep the king well protected during the opening and the middle-game, in the endgame, as this example shows, the king can be very powerful. Since there are few pieces left on the board, it is not in danger of succumbing to an attack so it can, and should, be used actively.

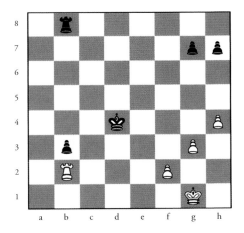

Black has a far advanced passed pawn which is supported by a rook. At the moment, White's rook is blocking the pawn's progress, but this can easily be dislodged by moving in the king:

1 ... Kc3

The rook is attacked so must move:

2 Re2

and the pawn marches on:

2 ... b2.

White will be forced to surrender the rook for the pawn, after which Black wins easily.

If White had been able to bring his king across earlier, he probably could have prevented this invasion.

In the next position, the attacking side is again using the king to support a passed pawn.

This is the most basic endgame that exists – king and pawn versus king – and it is more complicated than it might appear at first sight. Suppose it is White to play. The only way to make progress is to push the pawn forward.

1   e6

Supported by the king, of course, it cannot be taken. Black must now give ground with the king – but where to? Black must consider carefully. If he moves to one of three squares, he will be defeated, whereas one square will result in a draw.

1 ... Ke8 is the only one that draws: 2 Kd6 Kd8   3 e7+ Ke8   4 Ke6 is stalemate.

All the others lose. For instance, 1 ... Kf6 2 Kd6 (using the king to assist the pawn's progress) 2 ... Kg7   3 e7 Kf7   4 Kd7 and the pawn queens next move.

Or, 1 ... Kd8   2 Kd6 Ke8   3 e7 Kf7   4 Kd7 etc.

And finally, 1 ... Kf8   2 Kd6 Ke8   3 e7 Kf7   4 Kd7 etc.

This final position gives you just a taste of the complexities of the endgame. It is perhaps the most difficult phase of the game because you need to play with great precision and it is probably the part of the game which amateurs play least well. One of the best ways to practise the endgame is to set up all the pieces as at the start of a game, except leave off the queens.

PROMOTING A PAWN

When a pawn is promoted, the piece that it becomes is written in brackets after the move. For instance, if the pawn in the diagram (ABOVE) were to become a queen when it reaches the 8th-rank, it would be written: e8 (Q). If White wanted a rook rather than a queen, it would be e8 (R) and so on.

Competition Chess

Local and state chess tournaments are held at various levels all over the U.S. every weekend. Many lead to national tournaments. At a higher level there is a circuit of international tournaments played all over the world. If you decide you want to play on a serious basis, join a club and start playing in weekend tournaments (you'll have to bring your own board, men and clock).

TOURNAMENT RULES

In tournament chess, you will be required to follow a few extra rules and conventions. For instance, if you touch a piece, you are obliged to move it, and retracting a move is also illegal. Try to get into the habit of playing without letting your hand hover over a piece.

Another requirement is that you must record the moves of your games. Although this may initially seem inconvenient, with practice you will become more fluent so using the notation shouldn't break your concentration. The reason is not just so that you can go back over your games in retrospect. It is simply because most games are restricted to a time limit and a specific number of moves. For instance, in international tournaments, it is usually stipulated that forty moves must be played in two hours (the rate is much faster in domestic competitions), so you need an accurate record of how many moves are made. Players who fail to make the required number of moves within the allotted time automatically lose the game.

Special chess clocks with two dials allow the thinking time of each player to be gauged exactly. Immediately a player has made a move, he depresses the button on top of the clock; this stops his clock and starts his opponent's. At a rate of forty moves in two hours, this means that a move has to be made every three minutes. Few players manage to keep to such an even tempo, however. What sometimes happens is that the players leave themselves with only a couple of minutes to make a great many moves. Since it is essential to know the precise moment when the time limit is exceeded, all clocks are fitted with some kind of device, usually a flag, to indicate this. As it approaches the top of the hour, the minute hand raises the flag, allowing it to fall again when it has gone past the 12. Watching players up against the pressure of time can be very exciting when the clock is being hammered and mistakes made in haste. Sometimes a game becomes more a test of nerves than anything else.

GAMESMANSHIP

Not surprisingly, there is great scope for gamesmanship in chess, particularly when the stakes are high. As long ago as 1561, Ruy Lopez recommended placing the board 'so that the sun is in your opponent's eyes'. Shaking the table is a well-known problem. Most players are so wrapped in concentration that they don't even realize that they are doing it. The Petrosian-Korchnoi match of 1977 was a classic case. Little love was lost between these two players even before Korchnoi's defection from the Soviet Union in 1976, but at the time of this game relations had sunk very low. Korchnoi accused Petrosian of shaking the table while it was his turn to move, and fairly soon the main struggle degenerated from above the board to below it, and they began to kick each other. In the end, the organizers were forced to separate them with a partition under the table.

Staring at your opponent is an unpleasant – though regrettably fairly common – dirty tactic. One of the most celebrated offenders was Mikhail Tal, who was World Champion in 1963 at the age of only twenty-three. His gaze was so strong and powerful that it was said he could will his opponents into making mistakes. One Grandmaster even wore sunglasses to 'protect' himself. It is true that Tal's concentration at the board was particularly intense but, unlike others, he would never have done it on purpose and in any case he was capable of such strong moves that he did not need to resort to such behaviour. Be warned and try not to let anyone distract you from your game.

You can obtain details of chess events in your area by writing to:

U.S. Chess Federation
P.O. Box 3967
Crossville, TN 38557-3967

TELEPHONE: (931) 787-1234
WEBSITE: https://new.uschess.org/

Puzzles

Now that you have learned how to play, test your skills.
Can you spot the moves I made to win the following games?

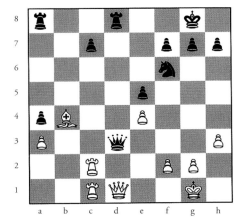

White, to play, may win
material by using a skewer.
How?

ANSWER ON PAGE 96

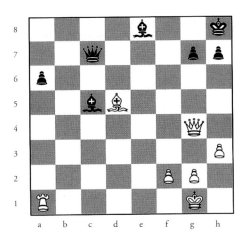

White, to play, has a simple
way to finish off the game.
How?

ANSWER ON PAGE 96

How can Black force a quick win?

ANSWER ON PAGE 96

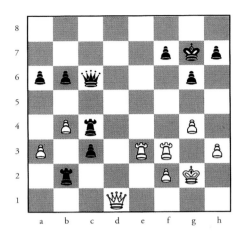

White, to play, may force a quick win.

ANSWER ON PAGE 96

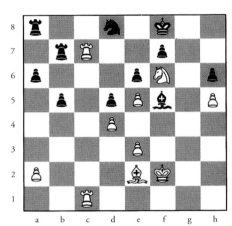

Black, to play, can exploit the pinned knight on d4 to win material.

ANSWER ON PAGE 96

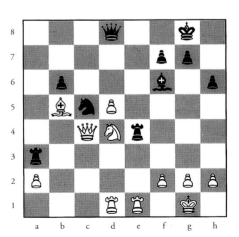

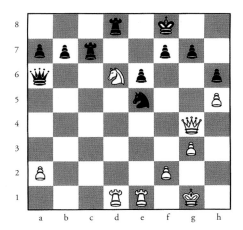

How can White conclude his attack? (This is not quite as obvious as it looks.)

ANSWER ON PAGE 96

INDEX

Many of the chess terms, moves and tactics in this book naturally occur in more than one diagram. This index will guide you to the initial or most detailed explanations.

ANSWERS

Page 27   FROM LEFT TO RIGHT a2, d5, f2, g7

Page 30   1 ... Nbd7

Page 31   Bxb7

Page 47   TOP 1 Qxh8+
The other rook is protected by the pawn on a6; the bishop is defended by the king; but there is nothing wrong with snapping up the rook in the corner.

MIDDLE (c) is correct. If the rook takes the bishop (1 ... Rxb5), then it can in turn be captured by White's queen (2 Qxb5). White will have gained two points. Taking the knight was perhaps slightly better, but still no bargain for Black: 1 ... Rxg3 2 hxg3 Qxg3. Black has won a knight and pawn (3 + 1 = 4 points), while White has won a rook (5 points), and thus wins a point. Neither capture is in Black's interest. There is no clearly best move for Black in the position, but bringing the rook back into the centre of the board with 1 ... Re5 does not look bad.

BOTTOM This is a slightly more complicated example. Capturing the knight (Bxg5) is not bad: it is an equal exchange; White neither gains nor loses material. But instead he may win a pawn by playing 1 axb6 axb6 2 Bxb6. White gave a pawn, but he won two in return. Notice how important it was to capture with the pawn first. If the bishop had captured first instead 1 Bxb6 axb6 2 axb6, White has won two pawns (2 points) but lost a bishop (3 points), so comes out down on material.

Page 58   TOP 1 Be5

MIDDLE 1 ... Bxh1

BOTTOM Blocking the attack is possible with 1 ... b5; defending the knight with either 1 ... Re7 or 1 ... Rc8 is also fine. If the bishop takes the knight, the rook recaptures, and this is an equal exchange.

Page 65   TOP 1 Qxh7 mate

MIDDLE 1 Qa8 mate

BOTTOM 1 ... Qe1+ 2 Rxe1 Rxe1 mate

Page 66   TOP 1 Qg4+ Kh8 2 Qg7 mate

MIDDLE 1 Nf6+ Kh8 2 Rxh7 mate

BOTTOM 1 ... Rh6+ 2 Kg1 Qh2 mate

Page 69   TOP 1 Rd5

MIDDLE 1 ... Bd4+

BOTTOM 1 Qe5

Page 71   MIDDLE 1 ... Bc6 The bishop attacks the rook which cannot move because the king would be in check.

BOTTOM 1 Qxg6+ The pawn cannot take the queen because the king would then be checked by the bishop.

Page 72   1 ... Rxf3+ 2 Kxf3 Bg4+ and Bxd1

Page 76   TOP 1 ... Nd7+ A lethal discovered check. After the king moves, Black's knight takes White's queen on b6.

MIDDLE Black's queen has strayed too far into the enemy position. There are plenty of ways to attack it, but only one way in which the queen can actually be trapped: 1 Rfb1.

BOTTOM Black wins a rook by using a discovered attack: 1 ... Nh5; White's queen is attacked so must move, and then Black's bishop takes the rook on a1.

Page 77   TOP By removing the bishop which was guarding the knight, White wins a piece: 1 Nxe8 Rxe8 2 Qxf7 (destroying the guard).

MIDDLE Black's a-pawn stands on the verge of queening, but at the moment White's bishop on e5 covers the critical square. By playing 1 ... d4+ Black breaks the communication. If White's king moves then the pawn queens; and 2 Bxd4 Nxd4 does not change matters.

BOTTOM Black's knight on f6 is overloaded. By playing 1 Rxd7 White wins a piece for if 1 ... Nxd7, then 2 Qxh7 mate.

Page 87   Any waiting move with the rook along the e-file (except e7 and e8) does the trick. For instance, 1 Re4 Kc8 2 Re8 is mate.

Page 88   1 ... Rc1+ 2 Rxc1 bxc1(Q)+

Page 93   TOP 1 Rd2 (If the queen moves, then Rxd8+ wins, so Black played 1 ... Qxd2 2 Bxd2 Nxe4 3 Rc2 and Black resigned. SHORT – KARPOV, SPAIN 1992

BOTTOM 1 Qe6 The only way to prevent checkmate on g8 is to play 1 ... Bf7, but then White will emerge a whole rook up: 2 Qxf7 Bxf7 3 Bxf7, with a simple win. SHORT – KARPOV, SPAIN 1992

Page 94   TOP 1 ... c2 2 Qc1 Rb1, forcing the queen to move and then the pawn promotes. SPEELMAN – SHORT, LONDON 1991

MIDDLE 1 Rg1 If Black plays 1 ... Rxc7 then 2 Rg8+ Ke7 3 Re8 mate. SHORT – SEIRAWAN, MANILA 1990

BOTTOM 1 ... Rd3, winning a piece. The game concluded 2 Nf5 Rxd1 3 Rxd1 Rxc4 4 Bxc4 Qd7 and White, having lost his queen, resigned. HULAK – SHORT, HUNGARY 1992

Page 95   1 Nf5. If 1 ... Nxg4 2 Rxd8 is mate; if 1 ... exf5 2 Rxd8+ Ke7 3 Qxg7 Kxd8 4 Qxe5 with a winning attack; or 1 ... Rxd1 2 Qxg7+ Ke8 3 Qh8+ Kd7 4 Rxd1+ Kc6 5 Qxe5 with a winning attack. SHORT – BAREEV, HOLLAND 1991